WITHDRAWN

JUN 2015

EMERGING
FASHION
DESIGNERS
5

Sally Congdon-Martin

Schiffer Publishing Ltd

4880 Lower Valley Road • Atglen, PA 19310

Designed by Danielle D. Farmer
Type set in BauerBodni BlkCn BT/Helvetica Narrow/Avenir LT Std

ISBN: 978-0-7643-4879-2
Printed in China

Published by Schiffer Publishing, Ltd.
4880 Lower Valley Road
Atglen, PA 19310
Phone: (610) 593-1777; Fax: (610) 593-2002
E-mail: Info@schifferbooks.com

For our complete selection of fine books on this and related subjects, please visit our website at www.schifferbooks.com. You may also write for a free catalog.

This book may be purchased from the publisher. Please try your bookstore first.

We are always looking for people to write books on new and related subjects. If you have an idea for a book, please contact us at proposals@schifferbooks.com.

Schiffer Publishing's titles are available at special discounts for bulk purchases for sales promotions or premiums. Special editions, including personalized covers, corporate imprints, and excerpts can be created in large quantities for special needs. For more information, contact the publisher.

Cover: Garments designed by Calle Evans. Photographer: Claudia Hershner. Hair Stylist: Jacqueline Root. Makeup Artist: Hannah Dorton.

TO MY DAD,
who is always brimming with good ideas.

CONTENTS

INTRODUCTION

In my opinion, a strong program in fashion design will not only nurture young designers' creativity, develop their construction skills and understanding of fit, inform their knowledge of the marketplace and the structure of the industry, and hone their unique point of view—the basics—the best programs will also provide the informed criticism, apply the pressure of high standards, and create an atmosphere of healthy competition to push designers past the limits of what they think they are capable of. In other words, a great program will create an atmosphere comparable to the "real world" of the fashion industry. Core curricula for fashion design programs typically includes pattern-making and draping, sewing and construction, textiles, design theory, fashion illustration, and costume history and covers everything from swimwear to tailoring to couture. The course of study generally culminates in a collection by the student designers that represents who they are as they enter the industry at large. This process of learning is very intense but, as you will see in the following pages, results in confident, prof-essional designers who are clearly ready to get out there and start making their names in a pretty unforgiving industry.

As with every edition, this year's group of designers continues to impress me with their creativity and the level of thoughtfulness and experimentation they put into their design work. Although they represent fashion design programs from across the United States, the newly minted designers in this book series seem to have much in common, most notably their fearlessness in pushing the boundaries of fashion design. Consider the textures and surface design created by Evelyn Jia, which are fully three-dimensional and literally "stand out," as well as Kelsey Greifield's use of googly eyes to instill a sense of euphoria in the viewer and David Valencia's futuristic interpretation of the traditional art of embroidery. The level to which shapes and volume were pushed by some designers is staggering—look at Alexandra Morgan Clinton's ballet-inspired collection, giving us all the volume of a tutu with none of the cliché, and Justin Chu's work, which defies gravity. These designers' minds are also open to unusual pairings. Sarabeth Fera successfully resolves a sort of Hawaiian print in a punk universe using the element of anarchy, while Michael Mann provides a hair-raising juxtaposition of fur and athletic wear and Amy Stolzfus marries crochet and neoprene. I am proud of the designers in this book for showing me things I have truly never seen before.

As with preceding editions, the process of selection began with the schools. I asked the programs to choose the designs and illustrations that best represent them, selecting from designers who mostly graduated in 2014 and are entering the industry now. Then I sorted through those submissions, selecting designers based on various criteria, including originality in concepts, exceptional construction and illustrative skill, marketability and, in some cases, all of the above. The work is organized alphabetically by school, with inspirations and materials for their designs listed to give a well-rounded understanding of their work. Additionally, the designers are indexed alphabetically.

The intent of *Emerging Fashion Designers* is to showcase the work of these dedicated young designers and to bring together the products of strong fashion design programs across the United States. I thank all the schools and participants who make this book a great showcase for emerging talent in fashion design.

ACKNOWLEDGMENTS

As always, I am so grateful to the supportive fashion design programs that participate in this project. There is much work that goes into gathering submission materials for consideration, and I would like to thank the schools and people that make the effort: Drexel University and Lisa Hayes, Cindy Golembuski, and Victoria Hurst; Fashion Institute of Technology and Judith Schwantes; Kent State University and J.R. Campbell; Massachusetts College of Art & Design and Sondra Grace; Miami International University of Art & Design and Charlene Parsons and Joleen Garcia; Parsons the New School and Sam Beiderman; Savannah College of Art & Design and Stephanie Thomas; Syracuse University and To Long Nam; University of California, and Davis and Susan Avila; University of Alabama–Tuscaloosa and Virginia Wimberley; University of Cincinnati and Margaret Voelker-Ferrier, Rene Schmitz, and Calle Evans; University of Wisconsin–Stout and Kathryn Kujawa; and Washington State University and Dr. Catherine Black and Bailey Marie Stokes.

I also would like to acknowledge the patience and supportiveness of my husband Jesse Marth — thank you. And to my editor Catherine Mallette and the designers at Schiffer Publishing—your guidance is, and has always been, much appreciated.

Finally, I would like to acknowledge the students and photographers who have allowed their work to be in this book. It is an honor to be able to create a forum to show your talents and creativity to the world.

DESIG

EMILY CARRELLO

DREXEL UNIVERSITY

Advised by: Lisa Hayes

Inspiration: The soft, curalinear forms found througout the architecture in Chefchaoven, Morocco inspire the silhouette, while the intricate tile work inspires the hand-embellished pattern of leathers and beads.

Materials: Marker, Micron pen, pastel and graphite with details in acrylic paint

Photograph by Emily Carrello

Materials: Rayon acetate, leather, glass bugle beads, metal beads

EMILY CARRELLO
DREXEL UNIVERSITY

Photograph by Emily Carrello

Photograph by David Gehosky

Materials: Silk charmeuse, 4-ply silk crepe,
leather, glass bugle beads, metal beads

Materials: 4-ply silk crepe, silk brocade, leather, glass bugle beads, metal beads

Materials: Silk charmeuse, 4-ply silk crepe, leather, rayon acetate, glass bugle beads, metal beads

EMILY CARRELLO
DREXEL UNIVERSITY

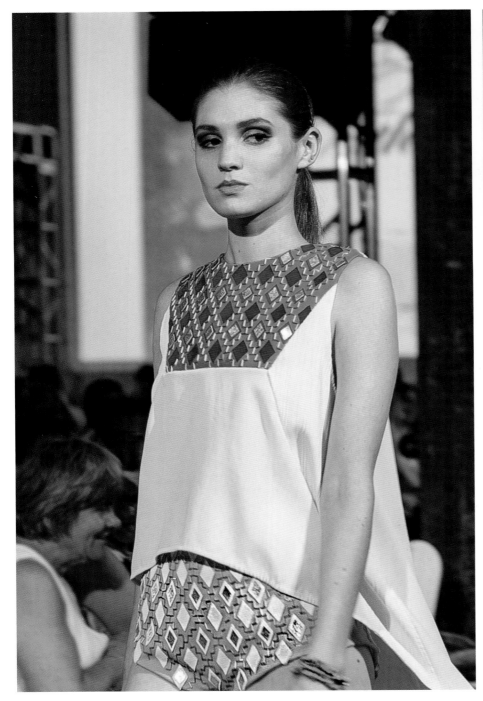

Photograph by David Gehosky

Materials: Leather, silk, glass bugle beads, metal beads

Photograph by Emily Carrello

Materials: Leather, glass bugle beads, metal beads

NEELAM CHANDWANI

DREXEL UNIVERSITY

Advised by: Lisa Hayes

Inspiration: Deriving the inspiration from Indian Henna designs, the collection is rich with cultural heritage in an attempt to add soul to fashion design. The designer is trying to achieve a perfect blend of technology, culture, and creativity to create a "Culturally Sustainable" collection. The intricate Mughal-era hand-embroidered Chikankari and metallic zardozi teamed with soft-textured experimental knitwear creates a delicate balance. Designed for the modern day fashionista who prizes history and has a quirky sense of styling, the collection strives to preserve the past, experiment with the present, and explore the future.

Materials: 3D printed earrings created with Rhinoceros® and Grasshopper® software

Materials: 3D printed jewelry

Shorts: Custom-made double-sided knit, with a blend of lurex yarn

Top: Created with hand-embroidered Chikankari procured from artisians in the villages of India

Photographs by Ken Yanoviak

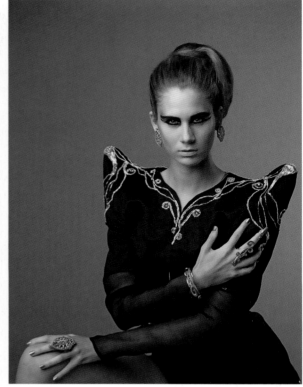

Materials: Cotton sateen jacket with zardozi-embroidered shoulders; 3D printed jewelry

Materials: Cotton sateen jacket with zardozi-embroidered shoulders, teamed with Chikankari hand-embroidered skirt and 3D printed jewelry

Materials:

Corset: Custom-made double-faced knit using both sides in panels and embellished with "dabka" and crystals

Pants: Black cotton sateen pants with zardozi hand-embroidered by the designer

3D printed earrings and bracelet designed with Rhinoceros® software

NEELAM CHANDWANI
DREXEL UNIVERSITY

Photographs by Ken Yanoviak

Materials:

Skirt: Custom-made knit embellished with "dabka" strands to highlight structure

Top: Zardozi-embroidered organza
3D printed jewelry

ARIELLE GOGH

DREXEL UNIVERSITY

Advised by: Lisa Hayes

Inspiration: *"Milan artists/design team Francesco Rugi and Silvia Quintanilla's projection of light wallpaper designs serve as the inspiration for my collection. Incorporating geometric shapes and the use of sheet textiles, the overlapping of color creates a bold and bright look. Leveraging this transparency, the primary colors red and blue and secondary color green produce exciting new colors. White plays a vivid role in my collection to help soften the bold colors and show the transparency of these garments."*

Photograph by A. Gogh

Materials: Silk organza, silk knit jersey, leather, beads

ARIELE GOGH
DREXEL UNIVERSITY

Photograph by A. Gogh

Materials: Silk organza, silk knit jersey, leather, beads

Photograph by Jeff Cohn @jeffcohnphoto

Materials: Silk organza, silk knit jersey, leather, beads

Photograph by Jeff Cohn @jeffcohnphoto

Materials: Silk organza, silk knit jersey, leather, beads

EVELYN JIA

DREXEL UNIVERSITY

Advised by: Lisa Hayes

Inspiration: *"My collection is inspired by modern architecture, both organic and sculptural forms. I explored structure and fluidity through the use of innovative materials, including precise laser cutting and 3D printing to create a three-dimensional form on the body. I chose a palette of shades of whites for a range of natural and man-made fabrics."*

Materials: Different weights of silk organza, as well as neoprene, wool crepe, silk chiffon, silk jersey, faux leather and the cotton polyester blend formite, which is specifically used for the white waffle surface decoration

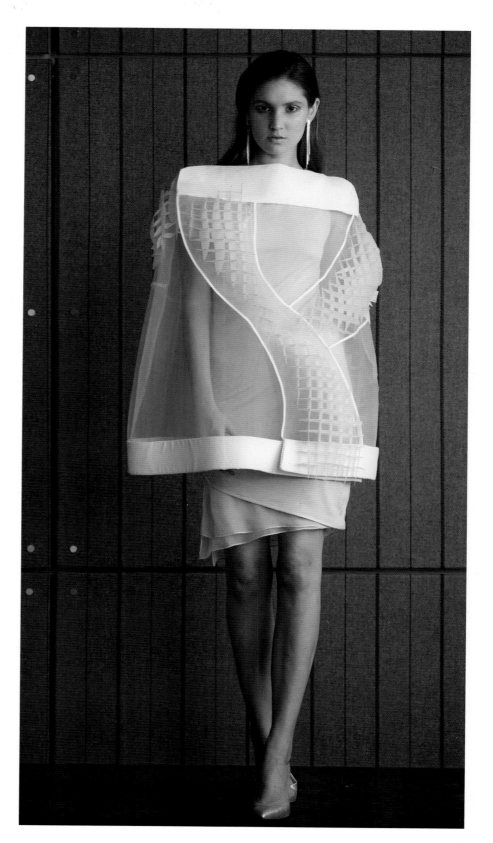

EVELYN JIA
DREXEL UNIVERSITY

Materials: Gouache

Materials: Different weights of silk organza, as well as neoprene, wool crepe, silk chiffon, silk jersey, faux leather and the cotton polyester blend fomite, which is specifically used for the white waffle surface decoration

Materials: Different weights of silk organza, as well as neoprene, wool crepe, silk chiffon, silk jersey, faux leather and the cotton polyester blend fomite, which is specifically used for the white waffle surface decoration

Materials: Different weights of silk organza, as well as neoprene, wool crepe, silk chiffon, silk jersey

Materials: Different weights of silk
organza, as well as neoprene, wool
crepe, silk chiffon, silk jersey

CASEY STEPHENS

DREXEL UNIVERSITY

Advised by: Lisa Hayes

Inspiration: "For my senior collection, I designed a women's outerwear collection for snowboarding. My inspiration comes from the symmetry of geometric shapes found in nature. Incorporated into my collection are my own graphic textile prints, which include both geometric and photographic prints. The garments also include quilting techniques, as well as fur embellishments in unique locations."

Materials: Illustrations drawn by hand, then scanned and re-drawn in Adobe Illustrator®, then filled with color in Adobe Photoshop®

Materials: 3M Thinsulate™ insulation, polyester poplin, faux fur, polyester diamond knit

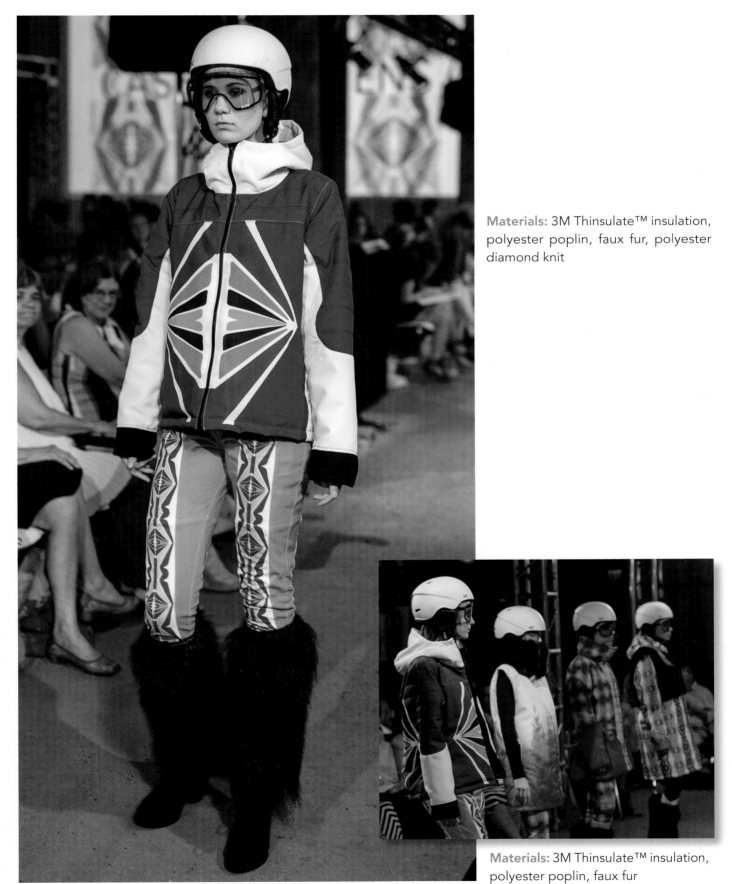

Materials: 3M Thinsulate™ insulation, polyester poplin, faux fur, polyester diamond knit

Materials: 3M Thinsulate™ insulation, polyester poplin, faux fur

CASEY STEPHENS
DREXEL UNIVERSITY

Materials: 3M Thinsulate™ insulation, polyester poplin, faux fur, polyester diamond knit

Materials: 3M Thinsulate™ insulation, polyester poplin, faux fur

AMY LYNN STOLTZFUS

DREXEL UNIVERSITY

Advised by: Lisa Hayes

Inspiration: "*The topical seed of my collection is character. During a women's jewelry project in Equatorial Guinea, I was asked a favor: come see the man's collection of sticks. He waved me down and persisted I see the many characters he had collected, inspired beyond their everyday function for the villagers. He let them journey through his imagination. In this collection, I started with an atmospheric color palette and contours, then allowed each look to breathe on its own. I have taken memories of my grandmother's Amish quilting groups and randomized geometries through individual shibori dye wraps, pottery crocheting, technological treatments, fabric manipulations, and the patterning of remnants. My focus is not technology or handcraft, but a biological journey of treatments that prototype personalities.*"

Materials:

Water Butler: Nylon filament neoprene, bonded jersey knit, 100 percent yellow wool double knit, anti-shock military-grade bungee cord

Photo by David Gehosky

AMY LYNN STOLTZFUS
DREXEL UNIVERSITY

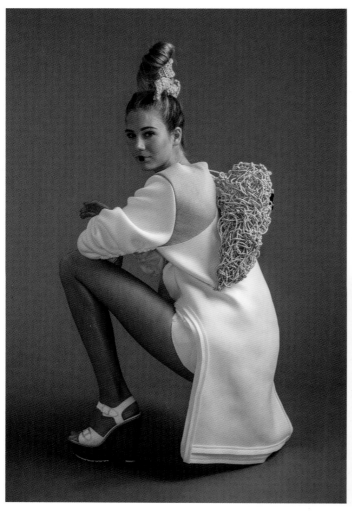

Materials:

Water Butler (female wearing unisex look): Nylon filament neoprene, neoprene pattern by-product, bonded jersey knit, anti-shock military-grade bungee cord, 100 percent wool double crochet

Materials:

Boundary Fencer: 100 percent double knit wool, bonded jersey knit, military-grade anti-shock bungee cord

Materials:

Bellows Handler: Nylon filament neoprene, repurposed and shibori-dyed nylon ripstop parachute fabric with original grommets

AMY LYNN STOLTZFUS
DREXEL UNIVERSITY

Advised by: Lisa Hayes and
Alphonso McClendon

Materials:

Evening Owl: rubber-bonded flesh neoprene,
engineered laser-cut nylon filament
neoprene, 100 percent silk organza, angora
wool, woven crochet chains

Materials: *Potters Niece:* 100 percent wool roving, nylon filament neoprene, neoprene pattern byproduct,

Advised by: Lisa Hayes and Sally Seligman

Materials: *Cloud Ringer:* Nylon filament bonded neoprene, shibori-dyed nylon ripstop parachute fabric contributed by Boy Scout group, anti-shock military bungee cord

TALISA ALMONTE
FASHION INSTITUTE OF TECHNOLOGY

Advised by: Brandon Sun and Barbara Kerin

Inspiration: *"The garments were adapted from my pre-fall collection titled 'Fragmented.' Geometric shapes, lines, and planes were the core inspiration of it, all coming together to create a harmonious mix of prints, patterns, and textures, resulting in a collection made up of many seams that strategically break up the silhouette into many fragmented parts. These fragments are placed in a particular way to accentuate the silhouette with patterns and textures that are repeated throughout the collection."*

Materials: Cotton twill, silk gazar brocade floral print, silk sheer blouse, Riri zippers/YKK zippers

Materials: Silk, silk gazar floral print, lamb skin leather, cotton wool blend, Riri zippers

Photographs by Osha Waiters

Materials: Cotton twill, silk, silk gazar brocade floral print, gray wool tweed, woven vinyl

Materials: Silk, silk gazar brocade floral print, cotton twill

TALISA ALMONTE
FASHION INSTITUE OF TECHNOLOGY

Materials: Jersey knit, lamb skin leather, silk gazar brocade floral print

Materials: Cotton wool, lamb skin leather, silk gazar brocade floral print, jersey knit, Riri zippers

Illustrations advised by: Steven Cutting

Materials: Colored pencil, pen, Prisma/Chartpack markers, pencil, Photoshop/Illustrator

Materials: Pen, pencil, Photoshop, scanned fabrics

SARAH ANGEL

FASHION INSTITUTE OF TECHNOLOGY

Advised by: Asta Skocir and Reiko Waisglass

Inspiration: "JOLT" is a collection inspired by the science of neurology and the concept of sensory overload. Brightly colored yarns in different weights are intertwined to translate the imagery of this concept into knitwear and to create a tangible expression of such intangible ideas.

Materials: 100 percent acrylic yarn

Photographs by Susanne Falch

Materials: 100 percent spun polyester thread, knitted and fused onto organza using Stitch Witchery®

Materials:

Top: 100 percent spun polyester thread, knitted and fused onto organza using Stitch Witchery

Pants: 100 percent cotton yarn, knitted and fused onto organza using Stitch Witchery, dyed with textile paint.

SARAH ANGEL
FASHION INSTITUE OF TECHNOLOGY

Materials:

Sweater: 100 percent cotton yarn, knitted with various novelty space-dyed yarn to give a random marled stripe effect.

Pants: 100 percent cotton yarn, knitted and fused onto organza using Stitch Witchery

Materials: 100 percent spun polyester thread, knitted and fused onto organza using Stitch Witchery

SARAH ANGEL
FASHION INSTITUE OF TECHNOLOGY

Materials: 100 percent spun polyester thread, knitted and fused onto organza using Stitch Witchery; 100 percent acrylic yarn, 100 percent cotton yarn and various novelty yarns used in embroidery of garments and knitted designs

DANIELLE ORTIZ

FASHION INSTITUTE OF TECHNOLOGY

Advised by: Alexandra Armillas

Inspiration: The designer used varied inspirations to conceptualize her lingerie designs. Geometric shapes and lines of symmetry inspire the first two looks in her profile. Her graduate collection, titled "Organic Chaos," was inspired by a modern art sculpture that combined a mixture of different elements, both modern man-made and organic materials from nature. And she is also inspired by vintage shape-wear silhouettes and gives them a modern twist in her third group.

Photograph by Alena Soboleva

Materials: Charcoal spandex with vinyl finish, light gray spandex

DANIELLE ORTIZ
FASHION INSTITUTE OF TECHNOLOGY

Photograph by Alena Soboleva

Materials:

Top: Jersey knit

Skirt: Matte black stretch satin, vinyl finish black spandex, black open-work stretch lace side panels

"ORGANIC CHAOS"

Materials: Marker, color pencil, Adobe Photoshop

"ORGANIC CHAOS"

Materials:

Bra: black leather and leather trim.
High-waist panty: Black leather and
power mesh, with black satin finish
elastics and garters.

Necklace: Black metallic lace

DANIELLE ORTIZ
FASHION INSTITUTE OF TECHNOLOGY

Materials: Embroidery on eggshell blue mesh, sheer beige illusion mesh/ spandex, sheer beige net, eggshell blue grosgrain elastics

46

Materials: Matte black spandex, Sheer power mesh, and black stretch lace.

Trims: Black satin elastic embellished with jet Swarovski crystals

Materials: Marker, color pencil, Adobe Photoshop

AMY TIEFERMANN

KENT STATE UNIVERSITY SCHOOL OF FASHION

Advised by: Dr. Sherry Schofield

Inspiration: "alt:unfolded" was inspired by a paper artist named Matt Shlian. *"Through my research, I eventually developed an interest in paper pop-ups. I made a life-size pop-up and draped it on the dress form to get inspiration from the shapes and silhouettes it made."*

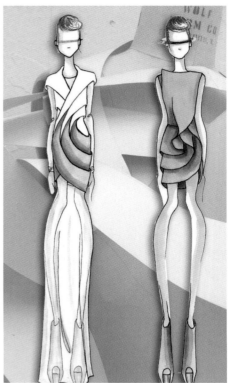

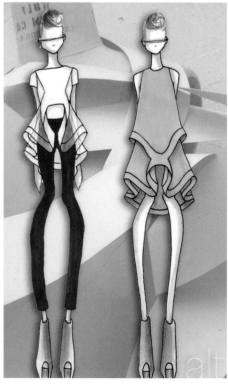

Materials: Copic markers and color pencils

Materials: Satin-faced organza, power mesh, silk zibeline

Materials: Satin-faced organza, power mesh, silk zibeline

Materials: Satin-faced organza, power mesh, silk zibeline

Materials: Satin-faced organza, power mesh, silk zibeline

NICOLE DIVITO

MASSACHUSETTS COLLEGE OF ART & DESIGN

TEXTILE PRINT DESIGN BY NICK SCHLERF

Advised by: Professor Sondra Grace

Inspiration: The inspiration for Nicole DiVito's senior thesis collection, "Steal Reserve," is college apartment living. The designer writes, "*For anyone who hasn't experienced this, it can be summed up as paying too much for the tiniest place infested with mice, bed bug scares, cold showers with clogged drains, living rooms adorned with cheap liquor bottles, and the consistent sound of sirens outside.*" Nicole used hand manipulation, material selection, and designed literal print motifs to convey the concept. She collaborated with Nick Schlerf, an animation artist, using one of his drawings inspired by Mission Hill to create a textile print.

Materials: Acrylic, graphite, watercolor

Materials: Digitally printed cotton poly knit, matte organza, hand-marbled cotton spandex blend

Materials: Digitally printed cotton poly knit, reversible fleece, matte organza, hand marbled cotton spandex blend, embossed faux leather

Materials: Plastic six pack rings, digitally printed cotton poly knit, hand-marbled cotton spandex blend

NICOLE DIVITO
MASSACHUSETTS COLLEGE OF ART & DESIGN

Materials: Bouclé wool, digitally printed cotton poly knit, hand-marbled cotton spandex blend, embossed faux leather

Materials: Digitally printed cotton poly knit, reversible fleece, hand-marbled cotton spandex blend,

Materials: Shower curtain liner, digitally printed cotton poly knit, hand-marbled cotton spandex blend, needle felted bouclé wool

Materials: Egg crate foam, digitally printed cotton poly knit, matte organza

NICOLE JIMENEZ

MASSACHUSETTS COLLEGE OF ART & DESIGN

Advised by: Professor Sondra Grace

Inspiration: Science fiction cinema and the SciFi graphic design style are the inspiration for this collection. The designer writes: "*My interest in SciFi and the city stemmed from being in New York. When I think of this place, I also think of the superheroes we see in movies. Inspired from this, I created my own story about a city named Glory—where the women are elegant, dangerous, and filled with wonder. As I researched graphic design styles, I noticed that triangles and crop circles were a common theme. I learned that the shapes can mean spirit, mind, and body; power intellect and love; and creation, preservation, and destruction. I felt that these themes relate to superhero stories.*"

Materials: Watercolor, ink, digital methods

Materials: Printed stretch denim, printed poly satin, leather, jersey, neoprene

NICOLE JIMENEZ
MASSACHUSETTS COLLEGE OF ART & DESIGN

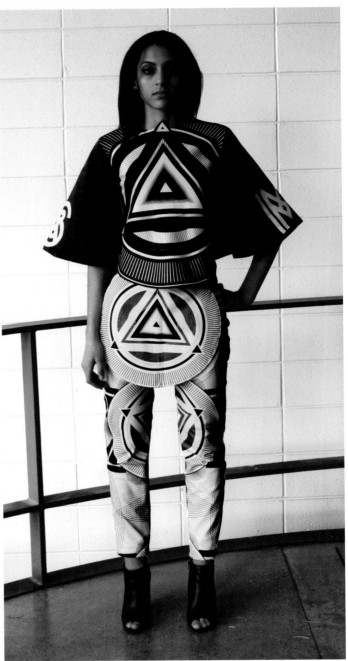

Materials: Printed stretch denim, printed poly satin, leather

Materials: Printed stretch denim, printed poly satin, leather, jersey, neoprene

Materials: Printed stretch denim, printed poly satin, leather, jersey, neoprene

NICOLE JIMENEZ
MASSACHUSETTS COLLEGE OF ART & DESIGN

Materials: Printed stretch denim, printed poly satin, leather, jersey, neoprene

JEONGEUN LEE

MASSACHUSETTS COLLEGE OF ART & DESIGN

Advised by: Professor Sondra Grace

Inspiration: "My inspiration is texture and fabric manipulation with a little bit of origami. Using some of my 3D paper cut outs, I wanted to try to fuse some of those ideas into my garments. My collection story is geometry and volume. I used fabric manipulation skills, such as quilting and tuck and fold, to make unique textures and geometric shapes. Because of the textures, garments can have volume and silhouette without any undergarment structures."

Photograph by Nikolas Rodriguez

Materials: Taffeta, satin, batting

Photograph by Nikolas Rodriguez

61

JEONGEUM LEE
MASSACHUSETTS COLLEGE OF ART & DESIGN

Materials: Taffeta, satin, batting

Photograph by Nikolas Rodriguez

Materials: Taffeta, satin, batting

JESSICA TENCZAR

MASSACHUSETTS COLLEGE OF ART & DESIGN

Advised by: Professor Sondra Grace

Inspiration: "*The Big Bang theory explains the sheer power and effect of physics, which aids in our study of where we come from and where we are going. This theory served as the inspiration for this cosmic and sublime collection. The clothes are for a strong and tenacious woman who loves a luxurious edge and unexpected touches.*"

Materials: Chiffon, croc skin, mesh, velvet, plastic, silk

Photographs by James Marquis

Materials: Chiffon, mesh, plastic, silk

JESSICA TENCZAR
DREXEL UNIVERSITY

Materials: Chiffon, plastic, silk

Materials: Mesh, velvet

Materials: Fur, chiffon, croc skin, silk

JESSICA TENCZAR
MASSACHUSETTS COLLEGE OF ART & DESIGN

Materials: fur, chiffon, croc skin, mesh, velvet, plastic, silk

Materials: Gouache

ERIKA WILLIAMS

MASSACHUSETTS COLLEGE OF ART & DESIGN

Advised by: Professor Sondra Grace

Inspiration: "Distressed Earthenware" is drawn from nature, art, and cultural heritage. The sun beats down against the ancient black lava cliffs, through dusty dry terra-cotta pastures, past humble white clay houses. Once crisp and clean blue and white azulejos are now worn and weathered. These elements of the Azores Islands seamlessly fuse together around strong tailored silhouettes to create a Spring/Summer 2015 day-to-evening ready-to-wear collection that features tailored white shirts accompanied by a variety of interesting textures and bold original prints—with all digital prints and accessories created by the designer.

Materials: Original print digitally created and printed by designer, linen, leather, linen/canvas blend, ultra suede, cotton/silk blend, wool knit, poly performance knit

ERIKA WILLIAMS

MASSACHUSETTS COLLEGE OF ART & DESIGN

Materials: Linen, leather, linen/canvas blend, cotton/silk blend, wool knit, boiled wool, poly performance knit

Materials: Original print digitally created and printed by designer, linen, leather, linen/canvas blend, cotton/silk blend, poly performance knit

ERIKA WILLIAMS
MASSACHUSETTS COLLEGE OF ART & DESIGN

Materials: Original prints digitally created and printed by designer, linen, leather, linen/canvas blend, ultra suede, faux ostrich leather, cotton/silk blend, wool knit

Materials: Prisma color markers, edited in Photoshop

Materials: Original print digitally created
and printed by designer, linen, linen/
canvas blend, cotton/silk blend

VESSELA YORDANOVA

MASSACHUSETTS COLLEGE OF ART & DESIGN

Advised by: Professor Sondra Grace

Inspiration: The inspiration for this collection started out with composer Graeme Revell. Revell uses insect sounds and a mixture of experimental instruments to capture the mood of night time. In this collection, two nocturnal creatures fall in love: the moth and the spider. The designer used fabric manipulation to create movement and illusion.

Photograph by Jillian Freyer

Materials: Jersey, faux fur, Lycra®, metal chain, fabric paint

Photograph by Andrew Swaine

Materials: Jersey

SEBASTIAN CUBIDES

MIAMI INTERNATIONAL UNIVERSITY OF ART & DESIGN

Advised by: Charlene Parsons

Inspiration: *"This look is called 'The Architect.' It was inspired by architecture and the use of new materials for construction. Nowadays, buildings are being constructed by new man-made materials developed with new technology, such as self-reinforced plastics, bio plastics, and electroactive polymers. This look was made of denim and cotton blend knit and plastic utility mesh. This plastic utility mesh is mostly what inspired this menswear look. It is normally used as protection from mosquitos in houses, but I realized that under strong light it resembles perforated leather. I learned that this material not only is capable of holding shapes that other materials used for clothing can't, but also is incredibly strong, and it lends itself to being sewn reasonably well....This material conforms to the body, reacting to body heat, and softens for unexpected comfort."*

Materials: Utility mesh, denim, cotton blend knit

Photograph by Orlando Garcia

SAMANTHA DE LA FUENTE
MIAMI INTERNATIONAL UNIVERSITY OF ART & DESIGN

Advised by: Charlene Parsons

Inspiration: *"The inspiration for the capstone collection I designed arose from the resilience of buildings and rocks that can withstand all types of weather. The color story portrays the different stages of weather damage, commencing from white then progressing to gray and finally ending in black. In this collection, I incorporated a variety of fabrics that have disparate textures and weights to represent the diversified ranges of levels and intensities caused by weather. Resiliency is represented not only by the damage inflicted from the weather onto the building but also in ourselves as we survive our everyday adversity."*

Materials: Leather, wool, jersey, plastic, yarn, canvas, tile separator, hardware embellishment

Photograph by Orlando Garcia

LARA LOPEZ-PICASSO

MIAMI INTERNATIONAL UNIVERSITY OF ART & DESIGN

Advised by: Charlene Parsons

Inspiration: *"My design was inspired by the Cévennes [National] Park in France. The beauty of nature and combination of colors made me create this garment."*

Materials: Bemberg, silk organza, brogue

Photograph by Orlando Garcia

ALI ROSE

PARSONS THE NEW SCHOOL

Photographs by Sam Gold

Advised by: Samantha Sleeper & Eliza Fisher

Inspiration: "*My inspiration came from my health journey navigating a diagnosis of fibromyalgia and chronic fatigue syndrome. I was encouraged not to be victimized by my diagnosis but to allow it to inspire my design process. I found beauty in the clinical spaces I was spending time in. My collection references these nostalgic environments through a muted-sterile color palette and textures that mimic hospital gown prints and outdated wallpaper. I reinterpreted historical nursing uniforms and infused functional details, such as cut outs in the interior of the arm on knitwear and jacket sleeves that unzip all the way, so that the patient doesn't even have to take his or her jacket off when getting blood drawn or getting an I.V. This collection is my declaration of victory over illness and failure. It is the physical manifestation of my healing—taking ownership of my creativity. Turning something painful into a joyful and humorous story of nostalgia and healing.*"

Materials:

Jacket: Laser-cut leather, cotton
Dress: Silk organza, re-appliqué, glass beads

Knit dress: Viscose yarn

Materials: Cotton knit sweater, Solstiss lace, wool skirt

Materials:

Left: Crepe wool suiting, leather hospital bracelet detailing

Right: Cotton shirting and organza, viscose knit lace motif leggings

OPPOSITE:

Left: Jacket: Mohair, Solstiss lace
Blouse: Pique cotton
Pants: Crepe suiting with Solstiss lace

Right: Jacket: Laser-cut leather, cotton
Dress: Silk organza, reappliqe, glass beads
Knit dress: Viscose yarn

ALI ROSE
PARSONS THE NEW SCHOOL

Materials:

Left: Vintage lace, cotton

Right: Cotton knit sweater, wool opera jacket, Solstiss lace, wool skirt

Materials: Viscose yarn knitwear dress

Materials: Cotton and polyester slub yarn lace motif sweater

ASHLEY YOON CHANG

PARSONS THE NEW SCHOOL

Advised by: Ruthie Kroah

Inspiration: *"My Senior Thesis at Parsons the New School for Design is called 'Thai Fisherman,' a collection for boys ages 8-16. It was inspired by my favorite childhood memory of always going fishing with my family when I was younger, combined with my fascination with the fishing and weaving industry of Thailand. I created my own hand-woven textiles on a loom and incorporated neoprene tubes in between for a more fun and modern twist."*

Materials: Nylon, merino cashmere, cotton

Materials: Nylon, cotton denim, merino cashmere, cotton yarns

Materials: Cotton denim, cotton

Materials: Nylon, wool, neoprene, denim

ASHLEY YOON CHANG
PARSONS THE NEW SCHOOL

Materials: Nylon, wool, neoprene, denim

Materials: Waxed linen, merino cashmere, cotton yarns, jersey knit

JUSTIN CHU

PARSONS THE NEW SCHOOL

Advised by: Fiona Dieffenbacher and Brigitte Conti

Inspiration: Justin Chu played with proportion, referencing the Arizona "waves" (sandstone rock formations) and the moment and spirit of the landscape, as well as Edwardian era details. The pieces conceal sensuality and find it through hidden and erotic forms. The designer expresses mysterious sexuality and uses the form of the dress as a metaphor for eroticism. Breaking all rules in draping, the panels wrap around the form and defy gravity.

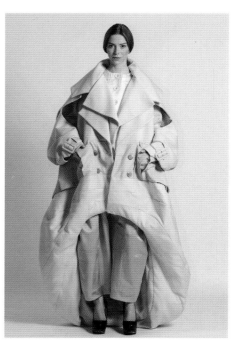

Materials: Microfiber gabardine, leather, silk wool twill

Materials: Silk wool gazar

Materials: Angora wool cashmere, leather, silk taffeta

Materials:

Overcoat dress: Microfiber gabardine, double-face silk charmeuse lining

Under dress: Silk organza, wool flannel, cashmere wool felt

Materials: Black double-face satin, silk taffeta lining, metal

BREANNE HARRISON-POLLOCK

PARSONS THE NEW SCHOOL

Advised by: Rachel Feinberg

Inspiration: "*This collection celebrates the strength in femininity. Power lies in being a woman, but society expects that women dress like men. With this collection I present an alternative. 'Woman does not exist without Man' is an exploration into clothing that preserves women's femininity, while reinforcing the strength they have always had. By combining elements of traditional women's wear and menswear, the construction of the garments becomes a representation of that dichotomy. The large silhouettes give wearers authority over their own body, allowing insouciance, and taking away society's expectations.*"

Materials: Cotton canvas, cotton shirting

Materials: Wool suiting, silk

BREANNE HARRISON-POLLOCK
PARSONS THE NEW SCHOOL

Materials: Wool cashmere, silk gazar

Materials: Silk gazar

BREANNE HARRISON-POLLOCK
PARSONS THE NEW SCHOOL

Materials: Cotton shirting

Materials: Canvas

INSEOP KEUM

PARSONS THE NEW SCHOOL

Photographs by Damien Wook Hyun Kimt

Advised by: Alla Eizenberg and Thomas Engel Hart

Inspiration: This Fall/Winter collection was inspired by the differentiation of light and shadows. The process began with draping a basic shirt, blazer, and coat. These garments were then photographed using a lamp in different locations to create new depth of shadow. These timeless silhouettes were impacted by the basic foundations of the shapes. Multiple layers of silk chiffon were established in the two-dimensional and three-dimensional elements from shadows. Inseop Keum strongly believes that the most significant apect of menswear design is to highlight clean and sharp lines. He also included the contrast of geometric lines and organic lines, incorporating feminine and soft fabrics, such as silk chiffon.

Materials: Silk chiffon, wool cashmere, silk cotton, pull-up leather, cowskin, wool, gunmetal beads

INSEOP KEUM
PARSONS THE NEW SCHOOL

Materials: Silk chiffon, wool cashmere, silk cotton, wool

Materials: Wool cashmere, silk cotton, pull-up leather, cowskin, wool

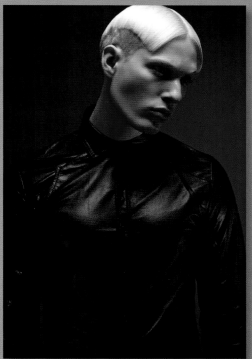

Materials: Pull-up leather, cowskin

Materials: Silk chiffon, wool cashmere, silk cotton, pull-up leather, cowskin, wool

INSEOP KEUM
PARSONS THE NEW SCHOOL

Materials: Cotton fleece,
gunmetal beads

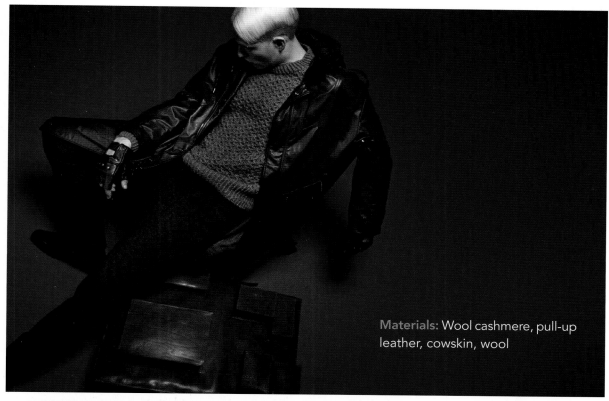

Materials: Wool cashmere, pull-up leather, cowskin, wool

Materials: Wool cashmere, silk cotton, pull-up leather, cowskin, wool, gunmetal beads

MENGRU LIANG

PARSONS THE NEW SCHOOL

Inspiration: *"Breaking apart to be put back together. Destruction and reconstruction. Upon visiting the excavation site of Pompeii last summer, I was completely taken aback by the remains of the buildings that were still potent and intact. I thought it was beautifully tragic, this idea of utter disaster and restoration, with the wounds still visible. I think my life is representative of these two paradoxes, where I have failed many times and experienced hardships but continue to mend myself and grow stronger each time. I titled the knitwear collection 'Mederi,' which in Latin means 'to heal, cure; remedy.'"*

Photograph by Mengru Liang

Materials: Wool and cashmere patterned knit, cashmere melange rib trim, wool twill, PinBond™ fusible

Photographs by Mengru Liang

Materials: Double-faced wool suiting

MENGRU LIANG
PARSONS THE NEW SCHOOL

Materials: Double-faced wool coating, wool and cashmere pattern knit, double-faced wool suiting, wool melange rib trim, PinBond fusible

Materials: Wool and cashmere patterned knit, wool melange rib trim, wool knit scarf, wool twill, double-faced wool suiting

MENGRU LIANG
PARSONS THE NEW SCHOOL

Materials: Wool twill, wool and cashmere patterned knit, cashmere melange rib trim, fine wool suiting

Photographs by Christin Ariel Pettibone

Photograph by Mengru Liang

Materials: Double-faced wool coating, wool suiting, metal D-ring closures, wool knit, PinBond fusible

MENGRU LIANG
PARSONS THE NEW SCHOOL

Photograph by Christin Ariel Pettibone

Materials: Double-faced wool coating, wool and cashmere pattern knit, wool suiting, wool twill, wool and cashmere melange rib trim, PinBond fusible, metal D-ring closures

mederi | fw 2014

by mengru liang

Materials: Colored pencil, marker, ink, Photoshop

KRYSTSINA SINKEVICH

PARSONS THE NEW SCHOOL

Advised by: Gabriel Asfour and Yoonkyung Yoon

Inspiration: This collection is based on the exploration of personal identity and influenced by [French artist] Claude Cahun's ideas. A grey linen coat was used for draping future pieces. Through cinching and anchoring parts of it to the body underneath with encased ties, loosely fitting silhouettes were created to evoke a sense of ambiguity between hidden and visible, just like the mask for Cahun participates in a dialectical play of revelation and concealment. From one look to another, the process of acquiring new appearances for that basic coat challenges the notion of personal identity being a unified entity, already prescribed for one by the society.

Materials:

Blouse: Crushed velvet

Pants: Wool blend

KRYSTSINA SINKEVICH
PARSONS THE NEW SCHOOL

Materials: Dress-coat with side pocket: Linen-wool blend with
hand-beaded embellishment at the neckline

Materials:

Skirt: Silk-wool blend
Wrap sweater: Various wool blend yarns

KRYSTSINA SINKEVICH
PARSONS THE NEW SCHOOL

Materials:

Top: Silk-cotton blend

Pants: Wool suiting
Wrapcoat: Linen

Materials:

Top: Silk-cotton blend

Wrapcoat: Linen

Hat: Various wool blend yarns

Materials:

Tunic: Wool blend

Wrap pants: Wool blend

KRYSTSINA SINKEVICH
PARSONS THE NEW SCHOOL

Materials:

Wrap jacket with side pocket: wool blend suiting

Wrap skirt: wool blend bouclé

DAVID VALENCIA

PARSONS THE NEW SCHOOL

Advised by: Sara Kozlowski

Inspiration: " '105 REASONS' is a personal journey I embarked on four years ago when I moved to NYC. My Senior Collection is inspired by personal memories and subliminal souvenirs I have carried around since the day I left home. The title of this collection is given after a gift I received from a friend. She wrote 105 reasons why she would miss me after I left Guatemala. It was the unconditional love that I found around me that drove this collection from ideation to development. It was about finding the balance between what you feel and what you think and how those forces complement each other."

Materials: Menswear cashmere suiting with machine embroidery details

Materials: Menswear cashmere suiting
with machine embroidery details

Menswear cashmere suiting
with machine embroidery details

Materials: Menswear cashmere suiting with machine embroidery details

119

DAVID VALENCIA
PARSONS THE NEW SCHOOL

Materials: Menswear cashmere suiting with machine embroidery details

KATHERINE ABSHER

SAVANNAH COLLEGE OF ART & DESIGN

Photographs by Raftermen, Courtesey of SCAD

HANDBAG DESIGN BY
ELIZABETH ROTTY

Advised by: Collection advised by Anthony Miller and Evelyn Pappas; Handbags advised by Michelle Quick

Inspiration: "*The garments were inspired by sculptural draping and classic tailoring. My collection combines traditional menswear fabrics with modern twists to create a uniquely feminine look. Always influenced by my British heritage, I became interested in using tailoring fabrics for draping and coordinating plaids into a harmonious story of scale and color. I then developed a foiling stencil inspired by boutonnieres and painted it by hand onto my garments. Supported by easy hand-knitted pieces, the woven separates can be mixed and matched to suit a polished yet modern wardrobe.*"

The handbag collection, titled "Resilience," is inspired by a story about a young woman who gets lost in the desert. The materials used largely reflect the woman's surroundings and struggles. Every bag is carefully hand-stitched with scarlet thread, echoing the story's theme. Python or water snake, hand-treated hardware, as well as a hand-casted logo complete each of the bags in the collection.

Materials: Double-face wool coating, hand-knit Lustra® yarn, black foiling applied by hand

Handbag: Python, water snake, hair on cow, nubuck, vegetable tanned shoulder calf, waxed thread, pig skin

Materials:

Top: Sequined wool bouclé with separating invisible zipper

Skirt: Harris tweed with leather trim and gunmetal buckles

Handbag: Python, water snake, hair on cow, nubuck, vegetable tanned shoulder calf,waxed thread, pig skin

Materials:

Top: Brushed wool tropical suiting with leather trim, gunmetal buckle and invisible zipper

Skirt: Merino suiting with invisible zipper and black foiling applied by hand

Handbag: Python, water snake, hair on cow, nubuck, vegetable tanned shoulder calf, waxed thread, pigskin

HANNAH AMUNDSON

SAVANNAH COLLEGE OF ART & DESIGN

Photographs by Marc Newton, Courtesey of SCAD

Advised by: Professors Marie Aja–Herrera & Carol Harris

Inspiration: " 'Delusions of Grandeur' was inspired by my generation's creation of 'selfie-culture' and constructing their image through social media and publicly posted identity. This obsessive self-editing and control over how we are perceived by others in an effort to make ourselves more 'likeable' is actually isolating us within ourselves, which this collection sought to understand. The garments are geometrically constructed with individual rhombus shapes and text and have mirrored, flat surfaces from the applied foil. These three looks say DELUSIONAL, SHAMELESS, and VAINGLORIOUS."

Materials: Organic cotton duck canvas, Pellon® ultra firm sew-in stabilizer, Heatnbond® ultra hold iron-on adhesive, Heatnbond lite iron-on adhesive, AMAGIC® textile foil in Autumn Gold, parachute cord, metal eyelets, Italian cotton shirting (lining)

Materials:

Jacket: Satin-faced silk organza, Haro adhesive, Heatnbond lite iron-on adhesive, polyester woven strap, metal parachute buckle, metal square ring, AMAGIC textile foil in Pale Gold and Bright Gold, Italian cotton shirting (lining)

Skirt: Organic cotton duck canvas, Pellon ultra firm sew-in stabilizer, Heatnbond ultra hold iron-on adhesive, Heatnbond lite iron-on adhesive, AMAGIC textile foil in Autumn Gold, Italian cotton shirting (lining)

HANNAH AMUNDSON
SAVANNAH COLLEGE OF ART & DESIGN

Materials: Satin-faced silk organza, haro, Heatnbond lite iron-on adhesive, polyester woven strap, metal parachute buckle, metal square ring, parachute cord, metal eyelets, organic cotton duck canvas, Pellon ultra firm sew-in stabilizer, Heatnbond ultra hold iron-on adhesive, AMAGIC textile foil in Bright Gold, Yellow Gold, and Pale Gold, Italian cotton shirting (lining)

JIAREN DU

SAVANNAH COLLEGE OF ART & DESIGN

Photographs by Marc Newton, Courtesey of SCAD

Advised by: Anthony Miller and Sachiko Honda

Inspiration: *"I was inspired by 1950s and 1960s women's beauty and fashion. I love their daily wear, their style, and their attitude. All I know about them comes from looking at '50s–'60s magazines. It really makes me imagine that if I could go back to the '50s, what could I design for those women? I could probably bring back some contemporary elements, silhouettes, colors, trims, and even constructions. In my collection, I used a bright orange, white, and pink color palette, modern shapes as garment details, and the fancy wool fabrics that create the '50s textures."*

Materials:

Coat: Double-face wool cashmere

Top underneath: 4-ply silk crepe; *lining:* China silk

Pants: 4-ply silk crepe

Materials:

Coat: Herringbone cashmere coating

Dress underneath: 4-ply silk crepe; *lining:* China silk

Materials:

Coat: Double-face wool cashmere

Top underneath: Novelty wool tweed;
lining: China silk

Skirt: Double-face wool cashmere

TINGTING FENG

SAVANNAH COLLEGE OF ART & DESIGN

Photographs by Marc Newton, Courtesey of SCAD

Advised by: Anthony Miller and Evelyn Pappas

Inspiration: This collection is inspired by movements of ballet dance and combined historical and modern ideas. The designer used pleats to create curves, emulating the plot development of ballet.

Materials: Silk wool, silk lining, netting, polyester boning

Materials: Silk wool, silk lining, netting

TINGTING FENG
SAVANNAH COLLEGE OF ART & DESIGN

Materials: Silk wool, silk lining, netting

KELSEY GREIFIELD

SAVANNAH COLLEGE OF ART & DESIGN

Advised by: Mark Hughes

Inspiration: "I was inspired by the feeling of euphoria. I wanted to make a collection that would make others smile."

Materials: Leather, polka dot flocked tulle, polyester sublimation illustrated print

Materials: Leather, neon vinyl, polyester sublimation illustrated print

Materials: Lavender calf hide, googly eyes, polka-dot flocked tulle

YOYO (LIN) HAN

SAVANNAH COLLEGE OF ART & DESIGN

Photographs by Marc Newton, Courtesey of SCAD

HANDBAG DESIGN BY
MINJUNG KIM (see next page)

Advised by: Collection advised by Denis Antoine and Evelyn Pappas; Handbag advised by Damion Le Cappelain and Michelle Quick

Inspiration: The garments were inspired by a very emotional moment and the understanding of life as a woman. The collection tells a story of transformation from innocence to confidence. In addition to being luxurious, the collection is very functional. Each look has one or more pieces that can be worn in a multitude of ways. The designer writes: *"This personalization and flexibility is a concept that is always at the core of my designs. Visually, the designs incorporate layers, which represent different stages in life and the progression from innocence to confidence."*

The handbag was inspired by Minjung Kim's search for a unique identity: The design aesthetic is minimal, edgy, and fun. Geometric shapes inspired the designer, whose design lines represent nontraditional and 3D shapes. The designer created the collection to represent her, and each product has a different meaning, including the pieces of laser-cut leather typography.

Materials:

Top: Tissue silk jersey

Bra: Imported mohair

Multiway-wear skirt/vest: Silver fox, mohair

YOYO (LIN) HAN
SAVANNAH COLLEGE OF ART & DESIGN

Materials:

Jacket: Silver fox, cashmere coating

Dress: double-sided wool jersey

Handbag: Designed by Minjung Kim. Oil tan cowhide, silver metallic lambskin leather, suede leather

Materials:

Coat: angora mohair

Top: Silk-like jersey, polyester mesh

Multiway-wear pants/dress/skirt: Silk-like jersey

CHRISTIAN L. HARRIS

SAVANNAH COLLEGE OF ART & DESIGN

Photographs by Marc Newton, Courtesey of SCAD

Advised by: Professor Mark Hughes & Patricia Trautman

Inspiration: Hemophilia and the belongings of the Romanovs inspired the collection. Nicholas II (Romanov) of Russia's heir had hemophilia, a bleeding disorder. The pattern cutting and silhouettes were inspired by complications of hemophilia, like joint swelling and failure of blood to circulate without interruption. The colors, details, fabrications, and embellishments were inspired by the imperial family who also hid valuables in their clothes when they tried to escape during the revolution. After their execution, the imperial family's belongings were stolen, burned, and/or thrown in a latrine pit. To that end, the garments in the collection were distressed. Swarovski crystals were used to suggest hidden valuables.

Materials:

Tank: Bleached, coffee-stained and broiled cotton/nylon blend rib knit with coffee-stained and broiled cotton rib knit trim, custom graphics (front and back)

Union suit: Bleached, twice coffee-stained and broiled cotton/nylon blend rib knit with twice coffee-stained and broiled cotton rib knit trim, twice coffee-stained and broiled linen plackets, bone buttons

Scarf: Bleached, coffee-stained and broiled cotton/nylon blend rib knit. cotton flannel interlining

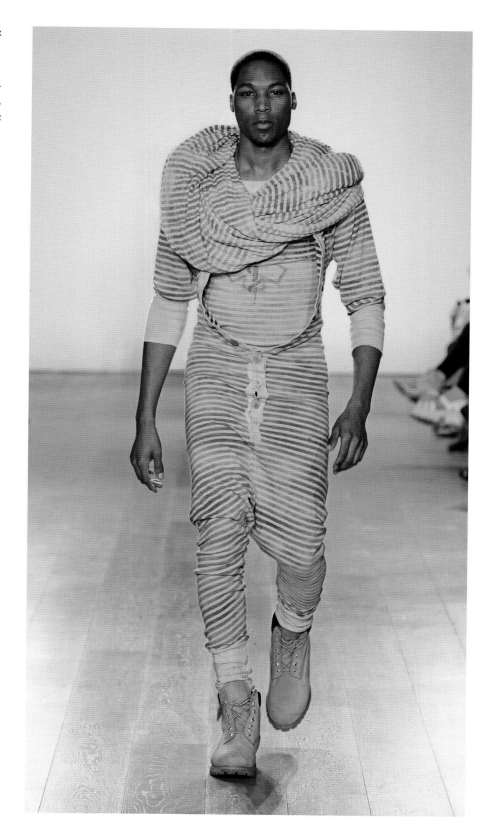

133

CHRISTIAN L. HARRIS
SAVANNAH COLLEGE OF ART & DESIGN

Materials:

Shirt: Coffee-stained and broiled silk/cotton blend chiffon with bone buttons, interlined (bib, collar, and cuffs) with custom newsprint hair canvas

Trousers: Twice coffee-stained and broiled herringbone cotton with cashmere back pocket appliqué, bone buttons, brass zippers

Materials:

Shirt: Coffee-stained and broiled 6-ply silk crepe with coffee-stained and broiled silk broadcloth collar, cuffs, and sleeve plackets; coffee-stained and broiled satin faced silk organza center front placket, bone buttons

Vest: Bleached, stone beaten, twice coffee-stained and broiled corduroy with coffee-stained and broiled velveteen back strap, bone buttons and hand mounted, custom woven Swarovski crystal swatches in areas where the fabric is worn away by stone

ELAINE LUI

Photographs by Raftermen, Courtesey of SCAD

SAVANNAH COLLEGE OF ART & DESIGN

Advised by: Sarah Collins and Stephanie Taylor

Inspiration: "*My senior thesis collection drew inspiration from the night scene in my native Hong Kong, with mesh-overlaid streetwear details covered with prints, LED light strips, and light–up LED details built into the clothes.*"

Materials:

Jacket: Polyester mesh, LED printed polyester twill, silver leather piping, polyester satin lining, ribbed knit

Sleeveless shirt: Pima cotton, silver metal buttons

Pants: Metallic spandex, ribbed knit, snaps

Materials:

Jacket: Polyester mesh, wax-coated twill, zipper, snaps, ribbed knit

Shirt: LED printed polyester, snaps, PVC

Materials: Vinyl, silver metal buttons

Tailored Shorts: Wax-coated twill, PVC vinyl, zipper, snaps, polyester satin lining

Biker Shorts: LED printed performance knit, elastic

MICHAEL MANN

SAVANNAH COLLEGE OF ART & DESIGN

Photographs by Marc Newton, Courtesey of SCAD

Advised by: Professors Stephanie Foy and Carol Harris

Inspiration: "My collection is about how we hide our true selves day to day in order to defend ourselves from the world. We build up layers of people and personalities that we're not, padding ourselves. We say mean things, try to dress and look tough. It's all about defense and guarding parts we don't want people to see, but exposing others."

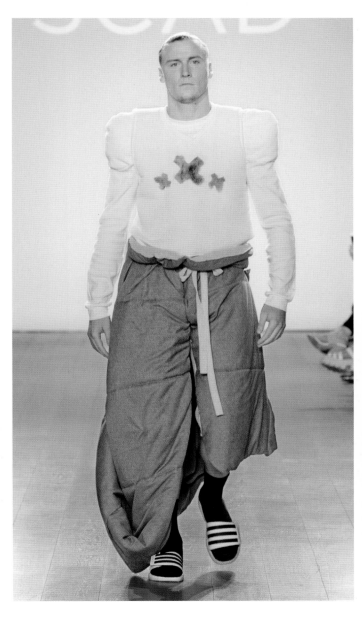

Materials: Sateen, coyote and fox fur, batting, fleece, cotton shirting, nylon ripstop

Materials: Spacer mesh, fox fur, rib knit, batting, poly/wool suiting, fleece

MICHAEL MANN
SAVANNAH COLLEGE OF ART & DESIGN

Materials: Spacer mesh, rib knit, fox fur, nylon ripstop, batting, parachute cord

LEAH MICHELLE SMITH

SAVANNAH COLLEGE OF ART & DESIGN

TEXTILE PAINTING BY JEAN-PIERRE VILLAFANE

Advised by: Anthony Miller and Sachiko Honda

Inspiration: *"I wanted to create a fun, energetic, and playful collection inspired by the art of graffiti; particularly, the graffiti that surrounds my hometown, Detroit, Michigan."*

Materials: Hand-painted silk/wool dress

Materials: Hand-knit baby alpaca wool sweater knit by Alice Cardasis Smith, wool felting, quilted poly-blend pants, knit jersey top

LEAH MICHELLE SMITH
SAVANNAH COLLEGE OF ART & DESIGN

Materials: Hand-knit baby alpaca wool
sweater knit by Sachiko Honda, wool
felting, silk/wool skirt

ALEXANDRA MORGAN CLINTON

SYRACUSE UNIVERSITY

Photographs by Joshuah Romero

Advised by: TÔ Long-Nam

Inspiration: *"My inspiration derived from the story of a ballet dancer whose expression comes through as she moves. She represents both grace and elegance, which embody the theme of my collection. Each dancer is essential to have a successful ballet production, just as each look I have designed complements my collection in its own unique way."*

Materials: Neoprene, vinyl pleather, silk crêpe de chine, silk organza, cotton satin

ALEXANDRA MORGAN CLINTON
SYRACUSE UNIVERSITY

Materials: Neoprene, vinyl pleather, silk crêpe de chine, silk organza, cotton satin

Materials: Neoprene, vinyl pleather, silk crêpe de chine, silk organza, cotton satin

Materials: Neoprene, vinyl pleather, silk crêpe de chine, silk organza, cotton satin

ALEXANDRA MORGAN CLINTON
SYRACUSE UNIVERSITY

Materials: Neoprene, vinyl pleather, silk crêpe de chine, silk organza, cotton satin

Materials: Neoprene, vinyl pleather, silk
crêpe de chine, silk organza, cotton satin

ALEXANDRA MORGAN CLINTON
SYRACUSE UNIVERSITY

Materials: Neoprene, vinyl pleather, silk crêpe de chine, silk organza, cotton satin

SARABETH FERA

SYRACUSE UNIVERSITY

Advised by: TÔ Long-Nam

Inspiration: "'The Outcrowd—Just the right amount of wrong.' My collection is inspired by the misfits, the rebels, and the outliers of society. 'Undermine their pompous authority, reject their moral standards, make anarchy, and disorder your trademarks. Cause as much chaos and disruption as possible but don't let them take you ALIVE.' —Sid Vicious"

Materials: Knit, cotton poplin, crêpe de chine

SARABETH FERA
SYRACUSE UNIVERSITY

Materials: Knit, cotton poplin, crêpe de chine, wool mohair, wool chevron, wool plaid, wool tweed

Materials: Knit, cotton poplin, crêpe de chine, wool mohair, wool chevron, wool plaid, wool tweed

SARABETH FERA
SYRACUSE UNIVERSITY

Materials: Knit, cotton poplin, crêpe de chine, wool mohair, wool chevron, wool plaid, wool tweed

Materials: Knit, cotton poplin, crepe de Chine

ALIX SADOWSKI

SYRACUSE UNIVERSITY

Advised by: TÔ Long-Nam

Inspiration: *"My collection, 'Baitogogo,' uses Henrique Oliveira's installation Baitogogo as a lens to view the transition from minimalist art to abstract expressionist art. What starts out as structural, linear shapes evolves into anthropomorphic knots and dynamic folds. Mixing shape and color, this collection has something that feels very architectural with organic references."*

Materials: Silk crêpe de chine, silk satin

Materials: Matte vinyl, neoprene, patent leather

Photographs by Drew Osumit

Materials: Matte vinyl, Neoprene, perforated leather, patent leather

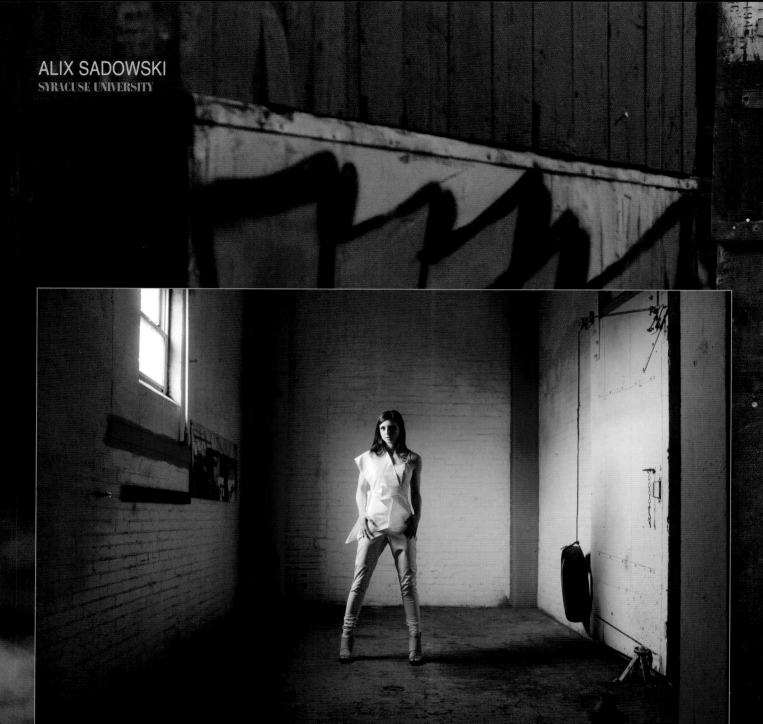

Materials: Matte vinyl, neoprene, perforated leather, patent leather, silk crêpe de chine, silk satin

Materials: Silk crêpe de chine, silk satin

Materials: Matte vinyl, silk crêpe de chine, silk satin

155

HAILEY SHELLHAMMER

SYRACUSE UNIVERSITY

Advised by: TÔ Long-Nam

Inspiration: "My collection, 'DEREZZED,' is inspired by the use of human anatomical lines with the integration of elements from cyborgs and robots shown through details—contrasting combinations between soft and technical fabrics, line, and texture all used to create a modern visual silhouette."

Materials: Silk organza, crêpe de chine, silk chiffon, silk satin, silk cady neoprene, vinyl

Materials: Silk organza, crêpe de chine, silk chiffon, silk satin, silk cady neoprene, vinyl

Materials: Silk organza, crêpe de chine, silk chiffon, silk satin

HAILEY SHELLHAMMER
SYRACUSE UNIVERSITY

Materials: Silk organza, crêpe de chine, silk chiffon, silk satin

Materials: Silk organza, crêpe de chine, silk chiffon, silk satin, vinyl

Materials: Silk organza, crêpe de chine, silk chiffon, silk satin

ELAHE SAEIDI

UNIVERSITY OF ALABAMA – TUSCALOOSA

Advised by: Virginia S. Wimberley, PhD

Inspiration: *"Ancient Egypt is back to life for turning mummification into the new black and white and glamorous. Different shapes of shoulder yokes reference the Egyptian necklace. I was born and raised in an Islamic country, [where] women are encouraged to use dark colors. Black and white are the colors that I have selected for [my] 'Black Queen' collection. Black is the predominant color of this collection to show women [as] elegant, chic, and sophisticated even in dark colors, and white represents the purity of women. The collection includes soft tailoring and structured dress and pants."*

Materials:

Outer shell: Twill weave polyester with black mesh;

Lining: plain weave polyester

Materials:

Outer shell: Black polyester with black leather- look vinyl;

Lining: Plain weave polyester

ELAHE SAEIDI
UNIVERSITY OF ALABAMA – TUSCALOOSA

Photographs by Elahe Saeidi

Materials:

Outer shell: Leather-look vinyl; *Lining:* Black
plain weave polyester

LINDA NGUYEN

UNIVERSITY OF CALIFORNIA – DAVIS

Photographs by Phillip Lee

Advised by: Susan Avila

Inspiration: Paper and fabric come together to create this structural garment inspired by the Japanese art of origami. Within the piece, bold constructed paper forms contrast with fluid, flowing translucent fabrics. The combination is meant to mimic the quiet meditative feeling of folding origami shapes out of crisp paper. Hand-painted disperse dye was heat transfer printed onto white fabrics to express dynamic linear motifs in vibrant colors, highlighting the actual folded lines in origami.

Materials: Chiffon and poster paper

LINDA NGUYEN
UNIVERSITY OF CALIFORNIA – DAVIS

Materials: Chiffon and poster paper

Materials: Chiffon and poster paper

Materials: Chiffon and poster paper

CALLE EVANS

UNIVERSITY OF CINCINNATTI

Advised by: Margaret Voelker-Ferrier

Inspiration: "La Jeune Martyre (The Young Martyr)" was insprired by the dark, eerie imagery of a beautiful young woman lying dead in her bathtub from the novel *Ice Princess* by Camilla Lackberg. What seemed like a beautiful, passionate love had a forbidden and darker side. The painting at the Louvre, "La Jeune Martyre" by Paul Delaroche, brought to life the imagery of what this collection represents. This scene of a murdered woman lying in a watery grave, so perfect with her innocence and beauty, is portrayed through each garment. The mood, the darkness, and the unexpressed emotion led her to this destiny.

Materials: Silk charmeuse, silk organza, vintage lace, silk chiffon, English wool, satin gabardine, silk ribbon

Photographs by Claudia Hershner

Materials: Silk charmeuse, silk organza, vintage lace, silk chiffon, English wool, satin gabardine, silk ribbon

CALLE EVANS
UNIVERSITY OF CINCINNATTI

Materials: Silk charmeuse, silk organza, vintage lace, silk chiffon, English wool, satin gabardine, silk ribbon

Materials: Silk charmeuse, silk organza, vintage lace, silk chiffon, English wool, satin gabardine, silk ribbon

CALLE EVANS
UNIVERSITY OF CINCINNATI

Materials: Silk charmeuse, silk organza, vintage lace, silk chiffon, English wool, satin gabardine, silk ribbon

KALEY MADDEN

UNIVERSITY OF CINCINNATTI

Advised by: Margaret Voelker-Ferrier

Inspiration: Inspired by the shamans of Eastern Europe and the German fluxus artist Joseph Beuys, "Trance" is an investigation into the relationship between the chaos of existence and the process of healing. It is an attempt to understand that you must integrate a crisis into the fiber of your being to become whole again.

Materials: Hand-woven yarns, leather, silk, jersey, voile

KALEY MADDEN
UNIVERSITY OF CINCINNATTI

Materials: Hand-woven yarns, leather, silk, jersey, voile, raw roving

Materials: Hand-woven yarns, leather, silk, jersey, voile

Materials: Hand-woven yarns, leather, silk, jersey, voile

RENE SCHMITZ

UNIVERSITY OF CINCINNATTI

Advised by: Margaret Voelker-Ferrier

Inspiration: "La Mariée des Fleurs" is a collection based on the essence of flowers. The designer proposes: "*The first representation of 'La Mariée des Fleurs' is the beauty and elegance of the shape of the flowers. The mind is then drawn to the meanings of the flowers and how the garments represent the symbols and words that characterize them. The colors are hinted at with a subtle indication for each represented flower. This collection represents my love of gardening and floral inspiration.*"

Materials: Silk duchess satin, charmuese, chiffon, China silk, habatoi, dupioni

Materials: Silk duchess satin, charmuese, chiffon, China silk, habatoi, dupioni

UMBREEN QURESHI

UNIVERSITY OF CINCINNATTI

Advised by: Margaret Voelker-Ferrier, Phyllis Borcherding, and Jacqueline Burris

Inspiration: " 'Pratipakṣa'; reframing one's perspective in order to regain balance. Growing up with an Eastern background in Western culture, I constantly sought out balance between the two worlds. A semester backpacking through Southeast Asia, Europe, and Africa showed me that as beautiful as each culture is apart, their infusion provides an even more powerful visual and cultural experience. This collection brings harmony to my opposing cultures through the use of Eastern silhouettes and sustainable textiles, which have been adapted for the Western eye."

Materials: All natural fibers collected while traveling. Silk, cotton and wool.

Materials: All natural fibers and stones collected while traveling. Silk, cotton and wool.

Materials: All natural fibers and stones collected while traveling. Silk, cotton and wool. Real agate beads.

Materials: All natural fibers collected while traveling. Silk, cotton and wool.

CASSANDRA BERG

UNIVERSITY OF WISCONSIN – STOUT

Advised by: Kathryn Kujawa

Inspiration: This collection was inspired by rock 'n' roll music and electronic music festivals. *"I have taken elements from my personal experience...with multiple music genres and created a collection inspired by the atmosphere and combining small details and elements of the two music scenes."*

Materials: Italian wool, leather, cotton/polyester, rayon

180

Photographs by Ben Hutchins

Materials: Italian wool, leather, cotton/polyester, rayon

Materials: Adobe Illustrator

ADDIE GECAS

UNIVERSITY OF WISCONSIN — STOUT

Advised by: Kathryn Kujawa

Inspiration: *"Bright colors and luxe fabrics were the initial creative inspiration for this collection. I also drew upon my Eastern European heritage, influenced by the desire to create clothes that could be cherished. Using exclusively all natural fibers, I explored artisanal techniques and fine tailoring to juxtapose crisp geometric intarsia prints with soft layers and hand detailing."*

Materials: Peruvian wool yarn, merino/alpaca tweed yarn

Materials: Drawn in Adobe Illustrator, and colored in Adobe Photoshop using scans of fabrications

Materials:

Coat: Cashmere double cloth coating

Skirt: Heather wool twill, silk twill; lining

Pullover: Merino/alpaca tweed yarn

Bag: Cashmere double cloth, wool; silk twill, genuine cowhide leather

Materials: Drawn in Adobe Illustrator, and colored in Adobe Photoshop using scans of fabrications

ADDIE GECAS
UNIVERSITY OF WISCONSIN – STOUT

Materials: Cashmere double cloth, wool coating, vintage Persian lamb, wool twill, silk twill, Peruvian wool yarn, merino/alpaca tweed yarn

LINDSAY LEY

UNIVERSITY OF WISCONSIN – STOUT

Advised by: Kathryn Kujawa

Inspiration: The designer was inspired by the countryside and by Greece to create "simplistic garments with hand details" in this collection, employing hand beading, hand knitting and seaming details.

Materials: Reversible woven print, 100 percent polyester

Materials: Reversible woven print in
100 percent polyester, and gold sequin
100 percent raw silk

LINDSAY LEY
UNIVERSITY OF WISCONSIN — STOUT

Materials: Woven print 100 percent polyester, sheer 100 percent polyester print and solid

Materials: Woven print 100 percent polyester, gold sequin 100 percent raw silk, sheer 100 percent polyester print and solid

Materials: White 100 percent acrylic yarn, gold beading, sheer 100 percent polyester print

Materials: 100 percent acrylic yarn, gold beading

LINDSEY FRANCES

UNIVERSITY OF WISCONSIN – STOUT

JEWELRY COLLABORATION WITH AARON WALLACE
(see following pages)

Advised by: Kathryn Kujawa

Inspiration: *"Color was a huge part of my inspiration, as well as experimentation with juxtaposing textures. This collection was inspired by classic romantic silhouettes with unique textural embellishments. I wanted to keep pieces natural looking."* The designer also referenced texture, flamenco, insects, and creating simple things with a high level of intricacy.

Materials: Patterned stretch knit, lambs-hide leather, birds-eye tulle

Materials:
Skirt: 100 percent gauze, hand-cut into strips

Top: 100 percent cotton, with upholstery tassels

Materials: Leather, recycled wool, silver fox fur

LINDSEY FRANCES
UNIVERSITY OF WISCONSIN – STOUT

Materials: Silk, wool

Photographs by Christopher Bartlett

Materials: 100 percent gauze,
hand-cut into strips

OLIVIA NELSON

UNIVERSITY OF WISCONSIN – STOUT

Advised by: Kathryn Kujawa

Inspiration: *"The name of my collection is 'Liv.' My inspiration came from my love of history and, more specifically, the early twentieth century. The ultra-feminine touches of that time and its organic forms were my key inspiration. I loved the idea of creating a modernized line that women can wear on and off the beach with fluid lengths and colors of shell, sand, and sky."*

Materials: Lycra, spandex, silk chiffon

Materials: Cotton, Lycra, spandex

Materials: Lycra, spandex

Materials: Cotton, polyester, Lycra, spandex

Materials: Cotton, polyester, Lycra, spandex, silk chiffon

OLIVIA NELSON
UNIVERSITY OF WISCONSIN – STOUT

Materials: Polyester, Lycra, spandex, silk chiffon

Materials: Lycra, spandex

TAYLOR MR WHITE

WASHINGTON STATE UNIVERSITY

Inspiration: The sweater twists the conventions of certain fabrics, and plays with the idea of weaving a knit. The designer was inspired by the way nature interlocks and interweaves. The shirt is a playful take on menswear, with each line of embroidery done "free motion" on an embroidery machine.

Advised by: Carol Salusso, PhD

Materials: Wool cashmere rib knit and heavy embroidery floss

Advised by: Patricia Fischer

Materials: Linen with cotton embroidery thread

INDEX

BY DESIGNER

ABSHER, KATHERINE

121

ALI ROSE

81

ALMONTE, TALISA

34

AMUNDSON, HANNAH

123

ANGEL, SARAH

38

BERG, CASSANDRA

180

CARRELLO, EMILY

10

CHANDWANI, NEELAM

15

CHANG, ASHLEY YOON

86

CHU, JUSTIN

CLINTON, ALEXANDRA MORGAN

CUBIDES, SEBASTIAN

90

141

78

DE LA FUENTE, SAMANTHA

DIVITO, NICOLE

DU, JIAREN

79

51

125

EVANS, CALLE

FENG, TINGTING

FERA, SARABETH

166

127

147

GECAS, ADDIE

182

GOGH, ARIELLE

19

GREIFIELD, KELSEY

129

HAN, YOYO (LIN)

131

HARRIS, CHRISTIAN L.

133

HARRISON-POLLOCK, BREANNE

93

JIA, EVELYN

21

JIMENEZ, NICOLE

57

KEUM, INSEOP

97

KIM, MINJUNG

131-132

LEE, JEONGEUN

61

LEY, LINDSAY

186

LIANG, MENGRU

102

LINDSEY FRANCES

190

LOPEZ-PICASSO, LARA

80

LUI, ELAINE

135

MADDEN, KALEY

171

MANN, MICHAEL

137

NELSON, OLIVIA

193

NGUYEN, LINDA

163

ORTIZ, DANIELLE

43

QURESHI, UMBREEN

176

ROTTY, ELIZABETH

121

SADOWSKI, ALIX

152

SAEIDI, ELAHE

161

SCHLERF, NICK

51

SCHMITZ, RENE

174

SHELLHAMMER, HAILEY

156

SINKEVICH, KRYSTSINA

109

SMITH, LEAH MICHELLE

139

STEPHENS, CASEY

26

STOLTZFUS, AMY LYNN

29

TENCZAR, JESSICA

64

TIEFERMANN, AMY

48

VALENCIA, DAVID

115

VILLAFANE, JEAN PIERRE

139

WALLACE, AARON

190

WHITE, TAYLOR MR

198

WILLIAMS, ERIKA

71

YORDANOVA, VESSELA

76